WHISPERS, SYMPATHIES, & APPARITIONS

WHISPERS, SYMPATHIES, & APPARITIONS

David Silverstein

Edited and with an Afterword by Paul Rossiter

ISOBAR PRESS

First published in 2014 by

Isobar Press
Sakura 2-21-23-202
Setagaya-ku
Tokyo 156-0053
Japan

http://isobarpress.com

ISBN 978-4-907359-04-1

Poems © Adam Silverstein, 2014
Preface and Afterword © Paul Rossiter, 2014

All rights reserved.

These poems have been selected from the books *Dazzled by Nothing* (Tel Aviv: Eked, 1984), *The Suspicious Sympathy of White* (Tokyo: Saru Press, 1990), and *Apparitions* (Ogawamachi: Jionji Press, 1991); some were originally published in *Americas Review, Chicago Review, Edge, Printed Matter,* and *Yellow Silk.*

With grateful thanks to Adam Silverstein, Nancy Baron *&* Jim McRae, for their help in making this book possible.

The photograph on page 77 is by Paul Rossiter.

Contents

Preface   7

from *Dazzled by Nothing* (1984)

Torrential Inconsequence   13
Nimbus   14
The Silence Shared in Crevices   15
The Clarity of Numbness   16
A Season   17
Allegiance   18
How to Draw Flowing Water   19
Cairo   20
The Laugh   21
Audacity Grows Wild in the City   23

from *The Suspicious Sympathy of White* (1990)

The Pig   27
Inviting the Hand   29
The Ignored Bird   30
Allowing the Manacle   31
The Importance of Moisture   32
Floating Ponies   34
Thinking of the Few Scattered Shells
      I'd Keep on My Desk Afterwards   35
Ruffians in the Northern Sky   37
The Interloper   38
The Brick   39
The Weather Sours and the Sweetness Is Good   40
The Walk   42

Invasion of the Room Snatchers	43
The Emissary	44
The Saint George Hotel	46
The Hunting	48
The Red Chair	50
Leaves	51
The Magnets of Paris Are Tired	52
The Surveyor's Nightmare	54
In Praise of Floods	55
The Reception	56
The Dry Teat	57
Talking Spoons	58
Deciding What to Do With Your Life	59
Living Alone	61

from *Apparitions* (1991)

Just Before Grass Is Reached	67
Dreaming of Fire, Waking with Burns	68
This Sadly Folded Day	69
Nothing to Unearth	70
This Heat	71
Winter	72
What Looking Sets in Motion	73
The Sadness When Water Withdraws	74
The Alley	75
Smoke	76

'Loving the Stranger': An Afterword on the Poetry of David Silverstein *by Paul Rossiter*	79

Preface

David Silverstein was a well-liked and well-respected figure on the Anglophone poetry scene in Tokyo in the late 1980s and early 1990s. Having already published his first book of poems in Israel before he arrived in Tokyo (*Dazzled by Nothing*, Tel Aviv: Eked, 1984), he published two more books in Japan: *The Suspicious Sympathy of White*, an eighty-page paperback published by Drew Stroud's Saru Press in Tokyo in 1990, and *Apparitions*, a small square book of twenty-six poems printed, according to the colophon, with a small cylinder proof press on *kozo* silver-fleck and mica paper, and with a cover of *momigami* treated with *konnyaku-nori*. This very Japanese object was created in 1991 at Richard Flavin's Jionji Press in Ogawamachi; '66 APPARITIONS are now realities', the colophon concludes.

Silverstein was a frequent attendee at the rather grandly titled Tokyo English Literature Society (TELS), in fact a writer's workshop held one Sunday a month in a municipal building in the Shinjuku area of Tokyo, and he often published in *Printed Matter*, the journal associated with TELS; he also published in *Edge* (another Tokyo magazine), *Americas Review*, *Chicago Review* ('Deciding What to Do with Your Life" in 1986 and 'Dreaming of Fire, Waking with Burns' in 1988, both included in this selection), and *Yellow Silk*.

After studying medicine and then obtaining a Doctorate in Child Psychology in 1974, Silverstein worked as a psychotherapist, at first in Israel, where, according to the back cover of *Dazzled by Nothing*, he used yoga both diagnostically and therapeutically. While living in Israel, be raised his son, Adam, from the age of eleven as a single parent; Adam, now an organic farmer in Colorado, speaks with great warmth of his relationship with his father, remembering him as 'a dedicated and loving father', and saying that he and David 'shared a love of language and humor and would leave each other long notes, spread across many pieces of paper full of cryptic and poetic musings'; they also both 'loved conspiring on practical jokes, solving logic problems, hiking and learning.' All these have continued in his own life, Adam writes, and have been passed on to David's grandchildren as well (personal communication from Adam Silverstein).

In Tokyo David worked first at the Tokyo Community Counseling Service and then at the Counseling Center of Tokyo, a cooperative English-language psychotherapeutic practice based in the Mejiro area of the city, until his premature and entirely unexpected death of a heart-attack in the spring of 1992. When he was working at CCT, he used sometimes to take his lunch in Mejiro Garden, a small municipally owned Japanese garden near the Center; this garden is the setting for the final poem he published, 'Smoke'. In this poem, the last one in *Apparitions* and in this selection, the gardeners – although they are not described – seem to have been clearing the underbrush and burning what they have cut back; rather uncannily, the poem turns out to be a poem of death and loss: the 'aged and beloved twig king has died and been cremated', and the smoke from his cremation passes over all the 'as-yet-unashed' inhabitants of the garden, who feel for a last time his 'benevolence pass over them as his hand once so tenderly did enfleshed.'

There is a photograph of this garden on page 77 of this book, following 'Smoke'; the dugout boat mentioned in the poem can be seen – although in fact it is a carefully placed dugout-shaped stone rather than a wooden vessel. This photograph, I believe, represents the setting of David's final poem; it also represents the view from the small building in the garden in which his memorial service was held on 9 April 1992, with readings of several of his poems, including 'The Importance of Moisture', 'Deciding What to Do with Your Life', and 'Smoke', all of which are included in this selection.

It has to be said that David Silverstein is an uneven poet, who perhaps wrote too much and too quickly. It also has to be said that the best of his poetry is very good indeed, and quite unlike that of anyone else (certainly quite unlike anyone else I have read, at any rate). I have a copy of *Dazzled by Nothing*, and I have copy number 34 of *Apparitions*, but I have never seen any other copy of either of these books; and, although *The Suspicious Sympathy of White* can occasionally be found in second-hand bookstores in Tokyo, David Silverstein's work has essentially vanished without trace. I believe that the best of his work is much too striking, original, and moving to deserve such a fate, as I hope this selection of his poems and the afterword at the end of the volume will demonstrate.

❦

The texts of David Silverstein's poems are printed from the first and only editions of his three books. Silverstein's punctuation is generally minimal and sometimes erratic; I have very occasionally added a comma or a dash when I felt that their absence seriously interfered with an understanding of the syntax. In his first book the spelling is British ('splendour', 'meagre'), but thereafter American ('rumor', 'center'); I have let this difference stand.

I have silently corrected obvious spelling or typographical errors. It was usually easy to decide in such cases: it seems clear that – for example – *fraility* (in 'Torrential Inconsequence'), *exhiliration* (in 'What Looking Sets in Motion'), *mastadon* in ('The Sadness When Water Withdraws'), and *emmigration* (in 'Smoke') were not intended spellings. In *The Suspicious Sympathy of White* the word *terseness* appears in the ninth line of 'Deciding What to Do with Your Life'; in *Chicago Review*, where the poem was first published, the word is *tenseness*, which seems more appropriate, so that is the reading I have adopted here.

One case was a little more tricky. At first I thought I ought to alter *whispy* to *wispy* in the last paragraph of 'Smoke', but in the end I let it stand: *whisp* is available as an alternative spelling of *wisp*; *whisp* can stand as a word in its own right meaning 'a slight puff of wind or sprinkle of rain'; and the word attractively combines *wisp* and *whisper* – all of which seem appropriate to the mood of the last poem in the book.

PAUL ROSSITER

from *Dazzled by Nothing*

TORRENTIAL INCONSEQUENCE

In the gutter the rain fears nothing
everything submits to the onslaught
the reluctant quickly change their mind
and the leaves long since dead
have a strange serenity about them
the joy of engulfment perhaps
flowing in the direction of what though –
mercy, rage, insistence? –
what is the point of the soak?
falling explains nothing
the awning above me reveals its frailty
i am the awning i am the leak
i am the rain
the sound is everything,
my heart suddenly hungers
only performance
even the cello's back
against the chair
satisfies something in me,
the drummer playing in my ear
carefully implanting his frenzy.

NIMBUS

And the lemons,
the unbitter lemons
are they imperfect
offending what we expected

and the ancient piers
that stick like tongues from the Levant
devoid of splinters or peddlers of fish
should we dismiss them too

the priests are silent in the lunchtime sun
the weight of the black gowns
and the forest of beards
circle the courtyard like self-intoxicated storms

thinking deeply of the lemons
heavy crosses on their chests
swing like lanterns for lost offshore souls

now even yellow it seems
must be walked like a bed of glass roses,
and the lanterns could be the eyes of anything.

THE SILENCE SHARED IN CREVICES

The tailor was deaf
and dumb and spoke
with the tip
of his silver needle:
finally precision

the stream with trout
flows entranced
my eyes too meander
for the bay: a calligrapher
of tact, he closes

a ragged tear in the back
of my black sweater,
black can never be discarded
silver and black and the end
of access, our seamless past

he wanted almost nothing for the work
sated with the secrets of my back
and the words he would never have to spill,
we looked at each other a last time
the words in his mouth the needle on the table
the hole an ancient rumor

THE CLARITY OF NUMBNESS

Here from several meters away
the view of the other is clear,
i establish myself
i take up residency in this place
avoiding the indiscretion of all theatre:
the frontal view

still i attempt to note everything,
favoring neither the hectic pronouncements
that pummel the inside of words
nor the islands of silence when breath
pursues a purer fate,
i see how the shape of the other wavers
i feel the small tides of intention and respite
and what with justice finally recedes for good

it is all there: the full weight
of what it means to be,
here several meters away,
beyond the blur of love –
the terrible nourishment of the aerialist
the thriving of unobstructed vision.

A SEASON

This would be the leaf's last flight
i watched it descend
exaggerating nothing
free of dramatics
without panic or fuss
it fell

i watched it free itself of hope
i watched it brush the ones
who shared a Season
those still green
and still able
to bend and weep

the falling continued
it seemed the others, renters all
sensed their own future now –
at the last moment
i looked away
i, so spoiled with seasons.

ALLEGIANCE

The dog sits at the foot of the boy
and merges with his shadow
together they wait for the bus
the bus waits on no one
the dog tries to be stone
and doesn't blink an eye
or move a single muscle:
a proof of something unseen –
and the flies who usually could
care less pause in their annoyance
sense something is up –
the dog with his silence
and his utter lack of movement
hopes to blend with the boy
like the stone of complicity
forever awed by the wall,
he will bend like a young tree
not agreeing or disagreeing
with what he hears or smells
until a second skin about him grows
like a wall of oiled glass

the silence serves as a moat
and all the bridges are consumed
with fire: only two words are needed
to make a sentence and but two souls
to form a country and the philosophers
debate whether a guillotine falling
in an empty room has really occurred
and whether the severed head
staring from the corner
was someone of principle.

HOW TO DRAW FLOWING WATER

Stand on one of the banks
hold a horsehair brush in your hand
and know that despite what you hold
the horse's spirit is still his own

until the water can trust you
she will reveal little of herself
so try to find out what it is
that water sees in life

look away from water
for she is everywhere in love with what she sees
only when she learns you are not from Rome
will she sit for the portrait you want.

CAIRO

If you need start with the lobby
and the scent of the bead clutcher,
start with a street scene if you must
or the rows of empty mail boxes
awaiting the magician or start with
the scars if you hunger for proof:
in the early mornings at even the smallest
of places you sidle over sagging floors
to a dining room full of tables for those
who never come: few do, alone, entranced
for first coffee and a foreign cigarette:
starched tablecloths spill lavishly
almost to the floor, mimic the splendour
of the bored tyrant, all done in silky silence:
perhaps a dress rehearsal for a new religion?
the waiters in floor-length gowns say nothing
to each other or the guests: they know what
needs doing: at last it happens, a question
swells within a guest and before the words
reach his lips, before the give-away is
given away, the look in the waiter's eyes
appeases what so agitates, embalms what
seemed so unresolved, flings discomfort
through the window like a conquered plague,
yes, here there is no urgency, this is Cairo
as it was yesterday before you came and will be
tomorrow when you leave or disappear.

THE LAUGH

The first year that the huge laughing woman had no effect on me i didn't tell my friends that i was someone else

she was a mechanical giant who stood before the Fun House

she was able to move her raised arms from side to side and her torso rocked menacingly from side to side too

not menacingly to we who looked on but dangerous to herself for she was precarious in her sway on the verge of fall tremulous with overweight

yes, close to tottering over, and if she did, we knew she would have been unable to raise herself again. she would simply lay there eventually giving way to weather or broken more decisively into more useful pieces

nor did we share this awareness among ourselves either, since some things are simply understood

being mechanical her frozen laughing face never changed its laugh and it was this look that hypnotized us: it was ambiguous

we assumed she knew what was behind it but we didn't, at times it seemed as if she were laughing in the face of some devil and thus trying to grin and bear some searing pain we were not privy to, an area beneath her painted wooden dress perhaps overheated, dare i say burnt from imperfect wires having eaten away at the lie of insulation. yes there were times that her laughing looked a poor cover for a cry –

and at other times the obvious stripped us of our meagre supply of courage, mocked our insipid burst of inches we brought to her each year. we felt that she looked down at us, ridiculed us, found our petty clawing approach worthy only of snide: despicable earthlings vulnerable soft-fleshed so ready to feel fear

but instead of evolving her laughter to more raucous and blatant humiliation, bursting into outright hysteria which she of course could not do and whose explosive purge would have relieved us, she persisted in her icy unaltered demeaning, and because we had no access to amends, no way of being verbally defensive with her, her insertion of constant jibe was that more painful –

at other times she seemed to say 'you are even unworthy of my falling on you – to crush you would be a fertilizing act a press upon that which I do not want'

why then plant for such a spring?

years later i heard she perished in the fire that consumed the whole amusement park and i read that she was the last object left standing before the onslaught, her legs ablaze her adornments fusing

i pictured her eyes surveying the fields, flames congealing everything, and beneath her laugh her huge bosom heating up.

AUDACITY GROWS WILD IN THE CITY

With what disrespect do these wild plants grow
through stone walls, through shadows
that themselves mock the artist's sketch
they move at will it seems
and not at the wind's beckon

with what disrespect do these bushes overheave
the barbed wire fences, rusted
and hoarse from shouting orders:
metal crying wolf has lost its rip
for the butterfly and bird

with what disrespect do these lungs surmount
steep hills when air is long since dispelled
with what grand respect does Jerusalem
blow in our faces the Alps and the oceans
and Spring in the twelfth year of our youth
and passing the tree line climbing,
the single fish swimming
from his first breath to his last

the infant makes a fist and smiles
and thus it is recorded –
'On the seventh day emboldened for the first time.'

from *The Suspicious Sympathy of White*

THE PIG

> 'There were lots of models. They belonged to a union for naked models. By Russian standards to pose naked it needs a lot of guts. Some were so beautiful. Each day academics drawing for four hours. Outside was winter, dark. Inside was light. Electric fireplace. Everybody sweat, model with sweat. A lot of noise. Russian pencil makes special noise, like young pig.'
>
> Vitaly Komar *&* Alexander Melamid
> *Russian Conceptual Artists*

The pig knew it was a pig and it knew of the moment's strange synchronicity. With the midnight sun, the eye is glad to work overtime. The pig made no bones about it. Its pigness. Its cheap vinyl exterior, the very slope of cheapness in fact. As if an interior befouled world were straining against the concave cage trying to flee from itself. Curves pressured to be Caruso every night.

But the pig's soul lay back. The palms were soft. The pulse, that of a pond in the center of Maine in August. With a blueberry mentality. The deep blue belief that in the hung one drop moment the sun's kiss would find it and solve everything.

But if it were shopping with friends – a tail muffler, ear-muffs, a negligee – it looked in the sparkling glass full blast. Pride. 'I am pig.' And it smiled. (By the way, it is hard, even in a city as sophisticated as this, for a pig to find heels. There is inevitably that crude remark by the salesman, 'Those feet,' or the opposite when from nowhere a pantomimed snort, the professed attraction, the unsolicited caress. The stockboy as pervert.)

And so it was with silken grace that the pig moved about the model's flank. An adoring pencil of light tracing the stripper's nipple. Aware of the artists at the same time it was aware of its own growing urge, the pig's flush must remain subliminal. Pink could not give birth. And thus it moved with care. And awe. And this haywire pulse. And what could only be called Pig Passion.

The nude model's crotch was very hairy. The artist loves contrast. The pig the bush. A weight of hair. A beckon of hair. An exquisite of hair. A pig trap? But isn't the manner of a sow's demise more matter than the death itself?

The pig could feel, among other things, in what was now a cauldron of conflicting fires, the pull of this Triangle of Glitter. The geometry of the pig's inquisitiveness was lost to sight. The pencils missed it though, the breeze missed it. The artists were not that developed.

The pig had become, in the slice of moonpie, a theoretical mathematician of lust. The pig licked the larger congruent triangle that ran from the model's knees to her navel. And using pig intuitiveness and a secret porcine shudder, extrapolated the smaller more exquisite bliss. National treasures are fiendishly guarded.

Outside, beyond the studio, Moscow snow, forever deepening. And still the blurring strolls of animators should the pig decide to glance. And beneath that frozen surface like a lost city of stone men, buried busts of Stalin.

Like huge slugs gathering strontium. Each one impervious to the now quite excited pig.

INVITING THE HAND

I felt closest to her when she was running her hand along the top of a table. Sweeping the grains of our making before her. The synthesis of everything spread was taking place. The disparate, once more believers. The words of the cat coalescing in the howl.

Night blanket. The hypnotist. The eye inducing the rest to lay down their arms. The retinal swallow.

I felt retrieval. I felt then what the wood must have felt. I wanted at such a moment a surface life, the ability for total surrender that only the flat have. I was so willing and yet devoid of will. Yeast on the run from itself.

Hillocks of crumbs she would come for later. Small fires left behind by a disappearing sun. Fond blebs on the horizon.

Nipples for the spirit to suck. The death dancer. What I really wanted was to make myself accessible to her sweep. Be the granular being I had not become.

THE IGNORED BIRD

The day grows unhinged. It is no longer a matter of light and darkness. There, in the lower sky of imminent dusk, a single bird is disregarded. The ignored bird thrives on something else.

Below, a woman sits on a stool by the station exit waiting for feet and the envelope of leather she shines for a fee. She sees how the body tapers and gives way to nothing in the end. She fights the sadness we do not admit to. She tends the pier with its abbreviated prosperity.

All about her, huge crowds blacken the sidewalk with intention of some sort. The swarm blurs her periphery like a city of errant stitches.

The ignored bird cannot exist on blue alone. It cannot stomach tampering. Sipping undefended hue is odious. A perversion of art. Someday it wants to paint.

The space about the woman is darkening even more as if from Delirium Crayons, and still the cool feathery line of the bird, so close really, rejoices: a strange balance of inequality.

And there in the wax cheeks of the shoe the woman sees one arc of the bird's flight like an unexpected life. Wings crossing shine, a desert of different limitations.

She sees what the bird is trying to do. It is trying to linger in the face of polish. The ignored streak thrives on something else. The woman lifts her soft cloth and moves for the neck of the bird, which the bird elongates for her strokes.

ALLOWING THE MANACLE

The high sheen of this black Sunday table is misleading. Though it has its arms out to light – it can sip it seems to say – when I touch it or rather when I slip from its arms, for that's what happens each time I try, I feel only a split-seconded chill, even a bitternesss.

The surface is bitter. 'I will not be fooled again by warmth,' it seems to say. 'Despite my blackness, this thick scurry of something pitch, despite my flat frontage on the bay and my attentive spelling of the sun.

Of all these other suns in the room, their hot loom, who beam their hot entreaties down upon me.'

It is possible then to find resistance even in the limbless.

I let my hand continue its slide. I do not halt its fall. Who am I to intercede in disillusionment? It clears the edge of the table. The few feet to the floor are behind it now.

And now on the rug my life is different. The pile is a simpleton who believes in loving the stranger. I too play dumb.

THE IMPORTANCE OF MOISTURE

I sat next to her on the train in the manner of two drops of water meeting on a shower door. There is something irresistible about a surface devoid of everything, as if matter, too, had its own supply of sadness.

Of course she was the perfect stranger, an ovoid insulated with blank pages and motive hiding from me effortlessly. I had no knowledge of what may have swayed her when the spirit wanders as she watches rain from the dry side of a window. The surface again.

Perhaps the very book in her hand, from which she never once raised her eyes, was a foil, a cloak meant to ward me off. She could not know of my love for theater. How for me a closed curtain is a rippling set of lips for which the only adequate response is trembling.

We both in fact were reading. I, a Proust essay on the Ephemeral Efficacy of Sorrow. It seems gratitude is in order for those who grant us pain. The morning fog enshrouding our hearts deep into the day, more like rocks than a fleeting melancholy, has been dispelled. Finally we see the heart stark in its solitude.

I did not want her, not even for an hour's conversation over coffee, but I admit to having been intrigued with the fantasy of our getting off the train together, entwined, leaving as partners, as if such deep involvement could spring fully bloomed and inexplicably watered.

But then I remembered that earlier in the morning I could not even get a stray kitten to drink from the bowl of chilled milk I had set out for it. A kitten who had been howling all night for moisture.

FLOATING PONIES

In the airport lobby where anticipated pleasures are forced
    into veins
as stylized sugar, a thin man
is assigned the task, hail his diligence! of dusting
a slowly rotating BMW
For this holy mother, dust is the incarnation
of evil, her vision is caked, the better world, her wrath
occluded, and dust on any groin turns love into a statue
Those barely visible flakes weaken the totem
and must be dealt with severely, they beg
a differing order: the longing to touch the earth with grace
    and silence
Somehow we must confirm our presence
without the aid of indentation
Think of the confused palm forever open and the unhorsed
    engine
Ponies of increasing smallness neigh
and remember the sac
Such animals need the sound and sweep of the falls
The thin man comes on the hour
A feather along the sealed spine of the BMW
Still the dust comes in seemingly endless supply as if it were
somehow reincarnated from the floor, from the feathers
like water like all things driven by persistence, whose spirit
is not diminished by fall but inspired to rise
In fact, if the thin man could see the tiny eyes of dust
he would see there an encapsulated registry of pure joy, small
white ponds content with the eddy
faces not unlike those of the swooping seesawers, first getting
then giving up, a somewhat suspicious laughter
when things are freshly loosened and set adrift and
the stomach is alone in the universe.

THINKING OF THE FEW SCATTERED SHELLS
I'D KEEP ON MY DESK AFTERWARDS

The woman who sells roasted chestnuts is a roasted chestnut. Somehow in the time warp between her flesh and my eye's gobble the change occurs. I see her through smoke, their common haze, and the churning of last resisters. There are always pockets of those who do not believe in history who think the missing limb is a passing phase.

She spends her nights in albums. She tries to imagine the tree before the nuts came, and her dream before it became true. To those who do not know, some of the pictures would seem barren. Not know of the later unfolding.

She does not smile.

If I could get close to her a roast chestnut smell the end of all other inhalations. If I could roll her in my hands the same stone hard feel smooth anonymous apolitical.

I would crack her in the end but her anguish would be brief. She and I would hover momentarily on the way to each other, I'd like to think that, or at least on the way to the churn, the second that gravel has with itself before the mixer.

She'd be there just beyond the last pouring strokes of small globes, that brief moment when distraction would be too much for her. And I'd be with the fleeting bittersweet –

That though I'd finally tasted the woman who sells roasted chestnuts I would not be watching her any more: not the pouring not the good sound of rubbing bunches nor her concentration nor the huge spoon nor the steam of transmutation nor her knowledge of just how wild to let the heat be.

The boarded-up booth her grave above the ground. The shells are flowers.

RUFFIANS IN THE NORTHERN SKY

About the prong-splay of my fork
The scattered crumbs of a poppy-seed cake
Are these, I wonder, corpii any less worthy
Of being constellations than the stars
Whose slow burn we endlessly admire?

Could there in this unmattered splatter
Be a message I cannot fathom still
Pattern of fled crumbs
Swirling in adoration
About an unsuspected center?

And should I dare
Lower my ear to the plate
Would a whirr of centrifugal libido
Sound there, a surface sex
Uniquely practiced by the fallen?

My eyes are blind, they see
Only a band of desperadoes
The last pocket of poppy toughs
Less than the dishwasher I feel
Who feels thru foam imperfect surface

Surrender to his sponge

THE INTERLOPER

The stone wall massively sloping was once pure unrelent. Created to be alone it is now everywhere covered in green fur. What shall we say, that stone has succumbed to moss or that moss has surrendered to the attractive brutality of stone, whose merciless presence the moss perhaps found irrresistible?

But neither would do, for yesterday has ceased to exist and naming the dead is a game for fools.

Rather we might say that in its willingness to mix, to be less than pure and give up its solitary life, green has matured, or that the huge stone has opened its fist and helped a stranger endure the pain of beauty.

A stirrup was offered.

But to talk of maturity in things that never die is a risky affair. It might be better saying, 'The stone dreamt its fur had turned green' or 'The moss had managed a muscle.'

THE BRICK

Away from stagnant setting days, from form's grazing curse, the brick grunts a way, the impetus implores 'away.'

Half on the curb and waist high the brick heaves itself up above the street above that crowd a wasteland of never before, on blind instinct.

What grand plans the stoney obese have!

What a day to ride the mount, to feel familiar fall away, to wed a softness with the help of something round, a wheel, a mammoth set of cheeks, cupping palms bringing liquid to a mouth.

Could this dream, machine, a set of gears whose clanks revel in the lift, be a friend the hitchhiking brick might ride?

Brick who wants to rise above its genes, fly like a brick!

The brick is a turtle among the hard, its small heart relentless in its small chest. Its one curve.

THE WEATHER SOURS
AND THE SWEETNESS IS GOOD

The wind whipping up hind legs fullest and then so alive fever pitch its death comes as a blow. A feeling of terrible loneliness. He could not remember the mood of implantation, the festive air that may have accompanied the manacle of seed to rut, but at this moment his mind was back there again entangled with roots when dirt was new and even worms young and gay.

The ends of a string remain strangers. They live through rumor of each other. Tension frenzy ripple and the occasional false passion of the knot, the electrical grip insuring the climber's greed: I want to lick the summit, I want to imprison the vista, I want to see the world from above as I do my cuffs.

He touched the table and felt recoil, the grains fleeing into themselves. He knew surfaces announced a litany of what he could never enter, a world forever cut off from him. They would always elude his desires, they would disrobe for him, allow the photo, admit to light and his fingers' promenade – but nothing more.

It was something he tried to do, he wanted people to feel there was a serenade of encase about him, not of moral perfection that would incarcerate him with solitude (though it did) nor with the sorcerer's heat which was equally moatful but rather with shell a wedding of whiteness reverberating, his whiteness wed to his whiteness and thus the guaranteed horror of the upper and lower lips who wake in the night thinking they are being kissed.

He wants to be born again each moment but not from a woman's groin reprieve but there – in a stranger's eye a magnificent style of inspiration and quite possibly the very sty of loneliness.

The realization: but now too late that only when the eye has been flushed could he have the shattering salvation that might set him free, the rid of egg. How he hated the thick ovals of the universe!

And so it was rain he thought of all day, thick inundations of it, drops that begot drops, a rain without end, a rain greater than the sinking of sin, a rain that would leave in place of the planet a single white towel drying in immaculate light, a rain that coalesced everything in its wetness, and that would especially pour down his forehead into the pleading buckets that were his eyes.

THE WALK

Ubud, Bali

It is midday's sun and nothing sane is out. I have chosen this time to hike the high path above the river I saw from the bridge and which goes through the terraced ripple of the rice paddies and high wild grass swaying like dry water. The stalks encourage me. Go deeper.

The trail is wide enough for one man, precisely my size. I appreciate the accomodation.

I sense a balance in the panorama as if the solid and sublime had apportioned all the 'cubits-of-made' in which to cultivate themselves. There has been a treaty or at least a tolerance. What differs is not evil.

The path climbs. I head for the house in a cluster of trees. Luka is there. Luka gives me tea. She gives me welcome. I do not know her. I know her. There are books here I would have chosen for myself. And the mats and the art and the view, the posture taken by the house. I don't remember calling ahead. Is it possible that my heart leads a private life of its own, a life even I don't know?

I sit and stare out over where I have just walked. Already the act of recovery with the soil still freshly raked with my prints.

A chicken struts at my feet. Above me a bee enters the home it has made in a wooden dragon hanging by a single thread. The wind playfully making it a little harder.

INVASION OF THE ROOM SNATCHERS

A squirrel shows itself on the path
and gives me a look.
Just for a moment we live
in each other's eyes I
am squirrel and the squirrel's
breath coursing through my lungs.
But then he dives for thick grass I
would look silly diving. My look
has not fooled him he knows
how far I still must go. For him
there is a hole he knows and
there is exposure. I with
a thousand holes leading nowhere
and covers of equal uncertainty
trying to fill a thousand rooms.
An advanced being cannot
admire a squirrel.

THE EMISSARY

San Francisco

On the steps of Union Square the woman with
    the rearview mirror
endlessly checking yesterday looked at me over
    her shoulder

in a small circle of treated glass where tame
    mammals float
she saw me flying towards her in the music
    of sunlight

running the clavicular checkpoints.
Chagall sent me, I said, I am

the sweet bird of yesterday
who can leave the ground at will, depart

it and swim in your compact. I can
distract your psychosis, I can

enter your eye like beauty like larvae.
The sun took us then

into submission
into that small room

where liquid makes reserve
a pointless affair

and the mirror and the pool
move for each other's mouths

and the birds overhead dance
their shrunken dance in glass

and anyone happening by
sinks in liquid's diary.

THE SAINT GEORGE HOTEL

Santa Cruz, California

Outside this hundred-year-old hotel invisible cowboys loiter the yellowing skin of stone. What we are seeing is the surface skirmish of those who pine for yesteryear. The good old sallow of time and sun and an unharried existence. The St George does not rush itself, not up its own steps nor now in my eyes. But a string of boxcars lassitude by.

The clickety box recite, the passing train bite.

Wrought iron fire escapes hang beneath open windows like metal cobwebs. The assumption then, too, apparently was 'Walk away from fire.'

A single ladder leads to the roof, a vine of something, and I am saddened. Why does the ladder always have to love despair so much, why does it always entice us with talk of what is up ahead and then roar off laughing when it sees us holding on to air?

On a second floor sill a small vase holds wildflowers, a minor intimacy that tames their boredom.

I picture the broken man I cannot see, he must be there in one of the rooms flung flat on the unmade bed by the furies, staring at the ceiling trying to catch his breath   his balance   a bug just stand.

Above him cracks in the ceiling start out boldly but then give out like dry riverbeds to stronger paint to the desert's contempt for the weak.

Go ahead, St George, whisper to the man, show him the proper placement of bones, how to hold the divining stick.

THE HUNTING

In the cavernous spaces of the hotel a man was being pursued. Paged in the old manner of flesh tracking flesh with bell and blackboard held afloat. A circumnavigating boy determined to find. It was for the boy, the hunter, not a hollow job lacking dignity. He did not see himself living through others. A piece of string knows that sense of self dismissal. He felt he was doing it for himself like a fisherman's fresh rejuvenation who will smile at the end of a day empty basketed with an afternoon's history of artful casts. A smile walking the pier away from the sea under a darkening sky.

When asked what he did for a living he would say 'I find people.' When the questioner heard that, his words stopped their surfacing. The boy liked the end of words for he, too, lived in a wordless place, but for the small sound hung around the celestial cow as it were, and the smaller private rub of placard against his stiffly pressed jacket.

The sign he was carrying at the moment had a name as usual, but no opening no lips. 'Mr Fnng.' The boy's mind passed slowly over the surface of the finest Italian marble looking for a crack, an imperfection that admits us. But there were no handles. He didn't know what he would say when he finally found the man.

The man, still with his back to the pursuer, raised his arm, somehow sensing the needs of the tinkle. The beckon had grown red hot. And when the man rose to face the boy he knew was there, the boy saw that the man had no mouth. Both were living far beyond alarm so there was no aghasting.

The man was clearly pleased at being found. He said this to the boy with his eyes. He wanted only the finding. For the man, the word 'enough' was a small pile with real meaning.

He had no interest in vowels, in the emotional whining of consonants who did nothing all day but exchange fetid breaths, little polyannas of depair.

The over-and-over resuscitations the man found infantile and primitive.

THE RED CHAIR

For weeks now I've walked past this red chair cast out on an empty lot, seen its red vinyl seat lying on its side, and for weeks I've been upset seeing it there.

How is it that this discarded chair can upset me so, how is it able to move me with its pain and loneliness, its stolen red life endlessly unveiled?

It is a swivel chair, or was. Once upon a time its red posture could shift according to mood. It could change what it saw. Maybe that's what upsets me so, how it cannot move now as if encased in ice.

It looks the same way, always, never swiveling for a child or a woman or the full feel of a breeze on its red face. Its stare is stiffly fixed on broken comrades, on glass. On a whole race of unwanteds.

Somehow it must learn to live off memory, the easy swivels of youth.

LEAVES

In the morning the leaves are swept. Or they wait. The extended broom is set free the always jackal and the leaves brought to the pile. Once a prisoner is taken there are no exceptions. The wind comes for my face. Clouds scurry. Birds frantic with excitement. Forego melody. Pure passion. The wings are good with the primitive.

Some leaves hide. The rare jackal is bored. The stone wall is pocked. The air is so clear before the burning begins that nothing exists between heaven and earth. The mouths of the gods abut our ears. The priests panic. Our earlobes are hot with breath.

Leaves in the gutter. Leaves in the form of leaves. I hide one leaf in my pocket and worry the crunch will give us away. It is eight A.M. in winter Saturday and a young girl is outside walking in a garden. It could not be called play. She is alone. She wears light clothes. Something I cannot see is warming her. In the plants and the flowers. She doesn't touch them. She doesn't seem to be looking even. Something else. Deeper. Row after row feel her passage. She seems to have crossed an invisible line, a wall, or at least dismissed the usual complement of limitation – skin, size, age, pain, sex. The repository of scents. An asylum of raw colors where no one need show the lunacy others measure.

At night the leaves are burned and the girl inside with the warm-blooded others passing herself off.

THE MAGNETS OF PARIS ARE TIRED

This woman whose thinness was veiled in unkempt red hair, a froth of self overwhelmed, or angry waves flooding her forehead with rage

this woman who just a moment earlier had spoken of succumbing to despair 'I will be swallowed yet'

suddenly came to life in her description of the blind boy and his grandmother on the train she rode and felt, in describing – that act – in describing his ghostly white skin, a peel of moon covering his nakedness, his fingers

moving along his grandmother's face, eclipsing her care, who can really trace gratitude adequately?

ten of them: a dance of touching but untouched porcelains, a gypsy caravan of equally tender virgins, the vacationing doomed among the world of hands, the endless indulgence of she-who-could-see-so-well, the private

will of ten bony spirits

revealed

but in describing all this, slowly and deliberately, this red being suddenly recovered luster, the snake had pulse!

the rest was inevitable, the pompadour retrieved its grace, the sea remembered its destiny, and the fish I could only imagine as being in the depths, sensed again the way back towards true north perhaps her thinness itself was an elongated slit, not a metaphor, allowing her passage into this new and brighter room

the cool tapered opening a set of chilled and stiff lips sliding along her belly, the clear hint of the more embracing life she wanted.

THE SURVEYOR'S NIGHTMARE

Again desire has reason to leave. At first I found her appealing, even provocative, standing against the door, caressing the door, she disseminated herself outward and down, a steady trickle of infuriating water. An arc of freshly melted flesh whose angle somehow demanded worship. And I was a wild flower whose dry tongue was just beyond the snow. But then I was startled. I saw her total lack of demarcation. Her skin was incredibly perfect. But frightfully so. So undefiled by identity was she that all possibility of terrain had been removed. She is a woman on whom I would be able to find no orienting mark were I to devote myself to her surface. Or by some turn of events, left stranded on her. In every direction outward from my panic, dunes of no demeanor. My disappearance would be thorough. I would be involved. I would finally move beyond this place. I would be dislodged from my composure.

IN PRAISE OF FLOODS

Our relationship is clear. We have decided to go so far. We can and do embrace. For example the privacy of an elevator is ideal for what we have. I usually lean my brief-case up against one of the padded walls. This frees both of my arms. She usually keeps her French shoulder bag on, since it doesn't restrict her in any way. I fit myself to her. It is really quite easy. Our arms repeat what our torsos do on their own. I'd rather not say, 'like fingers in a glove.' But the fit is triumphant.

I love the initial feel of concavity and how we do away with it. I want to spill myself into her, but of course I don't. This is part of our agreement. The clarity we share. We shall not play Fountains.

Sometimes our cheeks brush, our faces in the same place. But never the mouth. This is one of the limits. The moat of treacherous water. Her mouth is out of bounds and mine an equal dragon. A violation of something. I've never really had it properly explained but there must be a reason.

I guess our hands are pretty much free to roam as they please, though they seem to sense the arrangement and never let themselves go. The rules of our involvement are clear.

The mouth is out of bounds. I wonder though what would happen if the elevator stalled or if we did include the mouth. What would transpire were the moat crossed and we found ourselves in each other's mouth or even beyond.

Wandering up the River Tongue. Tracking the source down, as in Africa, as in the depths of her throat, where the earliest gush first intends itself upon the land.

THE RECEPTION

An old man has fallen asleep sitting up on a train. His graceful thickly veined hands are open naturally and curved upward on his lap. They are holding something I cannot see, cushioning a fall perhaps. How his hands deserve to be sketched and lingered over by the eye.

I imagine his hands each with a palmful of eyes in them, the resting globes blinking languidly. His hands deserve to be met on even grounds, met halfway on their own terms, the terms of acceptance, but who among us is so qualified, so deserving?

Now he has drooled onto his grey silk shirt. Two dark irregular blotches, spots of saliva that strangely do not spread and convert other fibers as expected. The neighbors' integrity is preserved. The need to water himself discreetly.

His sweating bald pate is rimmed by retreating hairs. He has started moving outward, away from his center. Apparently he has seen enough. Like the clouds when they part, he is making way for the moon, a thin sliver now beginning its rise on his ready and willing cranium.

THE DRY TEAT

In this terrible heat a woman walks towards me, arriving like a briefly perfumed cloud.

I weather her and hate the sense of endurance in my posture, my bearing of her presence. I want to send my back away, I want to banish its influence and be left incapable of guarding myself. The cloud wants nothing of insistence, and moves on.

My soil lacked the prerequisite parch perhaps. Or my indifference was too practiced.

Again it is memory from which I must suck, the small sexless mound in which my days are buried alive.

TALKING SPOONS

In a disfigurement of a solitude, these spoons on self display.

A small unintending series of spoons, an eros of what has been forged and then set free, homeless spoons as they would will it, three of them, run off like this, erect before the mirror in their finitude, nowhere repentant. It is we.

Are they smiling? They are, and yet the missing eyes are sad, though still and sperm-shot, the unpicked lot wilts, the death of a pond is will, doubly gagged. Light says something altogether different in each one of them. The scribbling inscribing silver foreheads.

The slippery hands of silver can hold nothing, neither impression nor philosophy. This emptiness could be luxurious but for the panic. 'We must find boarders for our concavities.'

We were led to believe that in looking this long we would know something to the core, but instead the usual waiver, the hovering fondnesses we know too well coming from the mirror. A sensuality that blessedly slips off into the sea. Praise the untenable fingers.

Drowning spoons perhaps. But nothing despondent for there is in the sink allegiance to form, the worthy silhouette remains, and more. And now the will to talk with salt is there.

Imagine the scratched glottids of such a dialog, and the gala of the confessional, freshly risen: A Concert for Depth and Three Spoons.

DECIDING WHAT TO DO
WITH YOUR LIFE

A roll is on the floor
it has not fallen.

Somehow it has gotten this far
from the plate and that fate undetected
the alarm has not sounded.

> 'A roll is loose
> a roll is making for the wall'
> not yet.

I feel its tenseness from here
its soft cheeks belie a racing pulse
of fear. This is not the Broadway pro
it would have us believe.

And if I got down on my knees
and carefully approached, I know
I would see tiny droplets of sweat
on what from here appears a forehead
of smoothly painted butter, what
else could lacquer be but ruse?

Time is against it too
so soon it must decide for which
exit to make, its crawl of destiny
as it were. How long can one roll
hold its breath? For when bread
breathes the whole world knows.

How long can its luck hold out
and avoid the clumsy kicks of
high-strung eaters whose gluttonous
twitches can still deal death blows?

Perhaps to be eaten would have made sense
death with dignity without blindfold
or confession of the stupid nostalgia
of remembering acre upon acre of friend
and family all sprouting for the Spring sky
all sun drunk and aspiring with that
ridiculous faith grain has.

LIVING ALONE

Again the unexpected lodge in which all of life is turned into a throat. Beneath ground the stalled train in the unwet vestibule. The saliva is gone. We can no longer swallow, there is no desire, as if all our intentions were ludicrous and we realized it simultaneously. Could this shaft be the long inverted finger of the netherworld beckoning, the invitation I have longed to find in my path?

Between stations where nothing is supposed to happen and only nothing thrives. The box conveying us rids itself of collusion. And for once we can revel in the truth: we are getting nowhere.

Outside, a single massive bolt becomes the sun. The lodger's pose again like stone's stare coming from a park. The drops of sweat on the train's window no longer gayly streaming with demise. They are suddenly stiff. Their salty curves seem forged and strained. They cling to the glass as they would to a dry lover in a parching bed.

On the cavern wall chalk numbers. I think of the drawing hand transferring to stone what matters most. But what could possibly matter here unless the end of time can be counted out? Chalk, whose infinitesimal breath recalls the miracle of the desert. And the darkness, the magician of spell, that somehow evades us in the end. In this place of stolen skies a moon would only fall.

And there in a half-finished ladder against the wall there is a quality of return, a grimace in the paralleling iron. Or rather the left ladder never meant to be seen, is seen and aghast. Like a calendar on which a bottle of ink has spilled and drowned our coming days – startled free of stain.

This ungodly place which should be a vertical drop but isn't, matches no station and thus on maps-of-aspiration does not exist, but we are here.

From where I sit I have only a partial glimpse of the drama, but is anything ever fully glimpsed? Even someone we love and want to see, for if there is interest the foraging eye stops and makes a home, or wants to. Only with a lack of interest, a perfect apathy, will the scan be fair, but finally even the divine gift of the painter deserts him. He can no longer look. It is overwhelming, the endless benedicting.

So does this one bolt overwhelm me. I assume its tightness. What else do such things have to live for if not the airless seal? Why not grant it that, an exquisite flushing pummel when surface loses reason and tries to salvage love from conclusion.

And so these irregular metals facing belly to belly are clasped, not roughly, but the adherence seems almost liquid in its merge. There is no need of ferric claims of 'loving unto death.' The days are simply met. One unpromised day unfolds the next in a centipede's languid stretch.

Suddenly I feel the desolation of the bolt, the terrible loveliness of such twisted loyalty endlessly waiting for a dawn that does not break. Its surrender to the wrench and strange appeal of rust on cheeks whose autumnal flush cannot be stroked. And the slow clouding over of the bolt's one eye until it huddles blind around itself each time the plunging beast returns. Engulfed by a terrible wind which demands the worship of held breath.

In such a world as this the howl is all, and dreams of lubricant derange a small metallic mind.

from *Apparitions*

JUST BEFORE GRASS IS REACHED

She was a waitress and he had seen her at her loveliest, in her most graceful pose. She had shuffled past him with her tray of tea on the way to the couple sitting out on the lawn beneath the gazebo.

On the way she had to step over the corner of a goldfish pond and then pass a few feet along a slick marble floor before she entered the dominion of grass. She knew from experience.

It was slippery, and in the same move that would take her free of the marble's subtle treachery, she wrapped one arm about a marble column to steady herself. She was not fooled.

He didn't know why but he was overwhelmed by the beauty of her arm's movement. So sure about the column. And the column there for her. For her wanting, and then just as needingly, her letting go of it.

DREAMING OF FIRE, WAKING WITH BURNS

A bicycle poses in a Japanese garden, so infected with serenity it imagines itself a thousand years old. It strains to reveal itself, to the light, to the moment.

In the window of the house a young boy, aesthetically precocious, with no set notion of what a garden is, or what a bike is not, sees what the bike is trying to do. The boy is overcome with sympathy.

And comes out to the garden and carefully prunes the handlebars.

These days there are galleries that would jump at the chance to do a show on agony, clever dioramas with femurs stuck in sand.

The Buto dispassion for what we do to each other.

THIS SADLY FOLDED DAY

The folded bedspread
on the white chair by the open window

has no real destiny

no arms.

    And though hundreds of its
pink fringed fingers sing
of a willingness without end

there is absolutely no hope
for any entanglement

no second singer anywhere.

NOTHING TO UNEARTH

It is Sunday and the vegetable stand is boarded up, but these barriers of overturned crates are a soft alliance, a matting hint, the no is yes, the city is yours.

But what after all can a penetrator do once inside but languish in embarrassment and fascia. Once in the taken body an unanticipated loneliness ensues. A melon drunk with overripeness lies discarded on the ground, a sprig of fallen parsley, sand from pickling brine, a spider hopelessly entangled with itself.

There is an unseen pulsing in the shed, like yeast at work, some truth is feeding here. The corrugated tin roof with its inexplicable endurance.

On one side an olive tree gnarls away at emptiness and shadow. A world of knuckles stuck to the side of nothing but themselves, like muscular pretensions. The balance of tree and shed is something they have made together, weighed with eye and thumb.

Even I who insist myth on everything stand back in awe. Just this once, the interpretation is inside out, a carapace, worn like an anthem on the chest, a scribble on a pyramid the common eye digests.

THIS HEAT

the common temptation to stop everything it is pointless all movement for movement is the escapee's hope and there is no hope but do nothing

lie down in the street in the elevator between the scapulae of strangers is a valley hope there must be a way of nothing

of being unattractive to heat for heat is the hottest of all and comes to drink it too wants a way out of its own skin cool and something frisky

it is that search which forces the fingers of heat on, those awful worms which have found us, seals its thick boots like wax like rags stuffing every orifice

for the terror of such heat is the end of exchange the very idea of access has ceased being in the world.

WINTER

from inside my warm room I hear a walked dog panting in the
    cold night air
i imagine the neck and the leash

i can feel the tense sinew, the rules of leather holding

the lack of a single knot known by the dog, if he could only
    entangle
his master in one, leave him tied to a tree, he'd flee, still collared,
for the moon

i think of the walks he'd take on the moon, the whiteness
    whipped up
by his paws and his snout, the dog trail
in the cheeks of the man in the moon

the long bones of the moon a puzzle for his canines

the third tide invented by his howl, the sea
swallowing his master, the dog in the moon
i'd see from my room.

WHAT LOOKING SETS IN MOTION

From high above on the train platform the old woman watches the young players playing tennis. The distance makes it all silent. Like watching screaming people being shot through a moving train window, or wolves without voice boxes trying to howl closing in on a lost sleigh hopelessly far from Leningrad. The encasings of chalk, the powdered edges of rectangular worlds. And the shifting from one to another like greedy infestations. The infected wolfbites are curious about their pink neighbours behind the curtains. They cross the yard.

The movement of the tennis players lacks reason in the eyes of the old woman. That the ball must be tracked and subdued, only this is clear to her. But its violation is invisible. Its sins must be those of spirit. Surely, the woman thinks, the sentencing was levelled elsewhere. What she sees is sometimes hooded.

The old woman is an accomplice. Or could be. Her slowness, calm, a threat. The ball finds encouragement merely in her presence. Suddenly, between pummels, the ball rises of its own accord and floats, gracefully in one liberating arc easily clearing the ten-meter fence. The woman boards the train.

Their reunion will occur later, more privately. When the woman can be closer and more animated, and the ball less distracted by its exhilaration.

THE SADNESS WHEN WATER WITHDRAWS

On the wide pavement where crowds now pass the treadmarks of last night's truck are fading. Partial curves only, a porous beauty, they feel their stain recede. They are losing their grip on things. The patterns are undrawn. For a while rubber was wet and was heard and drew itself across the face of the earth. If we dared we might have followed the trail. We might in fact have faded ourselves.

But now an ill wind has come, a wind of disavowal and the tires have been banished from speaking. From turning youthful minds. Even the moon seems somehow drained of enthusiasm. It is paler.

I am frightened by this easy erasure of a ten-ton mastodon. Now there are tramplers everywhere kicking up dust. How brazen they are in a crowd. They've put last night's horns from their minds.

I feel too a sadness in this withdrawal of water. The same sadness I felt as a child on the beach when the tide was out and the wetness was exhausted. And the sand crabs came out. I remember their small faces and the look of panic there when they thought they'd been deserted.

Their underground alleys were already caking over. The miniature deserts in their crab throats in which only the sturdiest of plants could ever hope to survive.

THE ALLEY

The alley is an enrapturement of demise, a bliss
of ugliness. The brutal dereliction of all hope.

The alley kicks me in the eye, sister temptress
to the vacuum on her knees begging exhumation.

The yodel of the throatless man.

The alley is everything I fear, spun into a single black
thread I cannot resist choking myself with.

The alley scares me with its pause.
I dread its plans for nourishment.

SMOKE

And from my portal, always the portal, a lotus pond imparts its ease, its casual lap bestirs on all things hard a sudden sense of doubt, 'Are we wrong?'

Until the rocks whisper of the spiders hanging by the thread upside down, reinventing the world, drawing it out from still-shots of the always born,

And smoke crosses the pond in a sweeping languid caravan of the moment's emigration: the aged and beloved twig king has died and been cremated

And all who lived within his realm, grass, pond, stone god, dug-out, butterfly, temple, monkey, frog – all the as-yet-unashed

Feel this one last time his whispy benevolence pass over them as his hand once so tenderly did enfleshed.

'Loving the Stranger':

An Afterword on the Poetry of David Silverstein

> *And now on the rug my life is different. The pile is a simpleton who believes in loving the stranger. I too play dumb.*
>
> ('Allowing the Manacle')

David Silverstein's poems are often records of powerful moments of seeing. Look closely at the world, he seems to say, and it begins to transform itself beneath your gaze: what you had taken to be a bland surface turns out to be alive with story, fantasy, dream or insight – although the boundary between whether the insight might be into the life of what is being observed or into the emotion and psychology of the observer is often intentionally blurred. In Silverstein's poems – especially in the prose poems of his second, and longest, book, *The Suspicious Sympathy of White* (1990) – we can read about, among other things, the sex-life of cake crumbs ('Ruffians in the Northern Sky'); the loneliness of a discarded swivel chair that somehow 'must learn to live off memory, the easy swivels of youth' ('The Red Chair'); the desire of silver spoons for the 'scratched glottids' of dialogue with the salt ('Talking Spoons'); or a break for freedom by a buttered bread roll trying to avoid consumption by 'high-strung eaters' ('Deciding What to Do with Your Life'). Thus, one of the strands woven into the fabric of Silverstein's work consists of a series of glimpses – sometimes scandalous, sometimes desperate – into the private lives of the inanimate.

This is fun, and can be extremely funny. But Silverstein's work in this vein is not just an access to a playful way of choosing to see the world. What makes his poems interesting and often moving is the fact that the voice in the text knows full well that inanimate objects do *not* have private lives. In 'The Brick', a brick is noticed in the street lying 'half on the curb'; the narrator in the poem infers that it has 'heave[d] itself above the street' in an attempt to escape 'from stagnant setting days' and the 'curse' of its unalterable form. The narrator enters in imagination into the brick's hopes and desires – 'What a day to ride the mount, to feel familiar fall away, to wed a softness with the help of something round' – and asks, 'Could this dream ... be a friend the hitchhiking brick might ride?' He then exclaims: 'Brick who wants to rise above its genes, fly like a brick!'

It is difficult to know, in terms of the fiction of the poem, whether this is an act of generous encouragement to a being hemmed in by intolerably restricting circumstances and courageously striving to better its condition or – bricks having neither genes nor wings – a joke at the brick's expense. And is it, anyway, a brick we're talking of here? Is the brick not rather an emblem of human lives prevented because of their circumstances and nature – and despite their yearning for liberation – from transcending the curse of limitation? Or is the brick operating satirically in the poem to highlight the absurdity of the gap between the dreams of human beings and the limitations of their possibly brick-like nature? ('What grand plans the stony obese have!' the narrator exclaims at one point.)

The answer is, I think, all of these, and it is this that gives the poem its complexity: its portrait of the brick is simultaneously a portrait of an irredeemably physical object (in the spirit of the early work of Francis Ponge, perhaps) and of the Unknown and Much-Put-Upon Citizen; it is both an articulation of entrapment and a wry comment on human pretension, and in the complexity of its response the poem hints at the tragic, as well as being both touching and funny. The poem ends: 'The brick is a turtle among the hard, its small heart relentless in its small chest. Its one curve.' Here all the responses to the brick (and to the human beings the brick might stand for) are brought together as the dichotomy between the human and the inanimate is reconciled in the image of the turtle, the animate creature the brick most resembles. The turtle is limited by its genes, and by the evolutionary success of its defensive armour, to a single shape but in the poem is nevertheless respected, is found brave and touching both in its aspirations and in its failure to realise those aspirations.

The act of looking at objects in the world and transforming them in ways that they themselves might wish for and understand, while at the same time recognising that the objects themselves remain unaffected by this act of attention, and indeed that the transformation inevitably reveals more about the observer than the observed, is close to the heart of Silverstein's project. A surface is a surface is a surface, the brick remains a brick, and it is in fact 'the eye's rapid encroachment' that is 'the real cause of reality's swirl', the actual initiator of 'the indecent exposure of transmutation' (from 'A Mossy Wall', a poem not included in this selection).

The eye's rapid encroachment is sometimes simply a matter of anthropomorphic projection onto an inanimate object, as in the previously mentioned 'The Red Chair', in which the narrator describes a swivel chair that has been discarded on an empty lot and asks how it is that this chair is 'able to move me with its pain and loneliness, its stolen red life endlessly unveiled.' The answer is that 'once upon a time its red posture could shift according to mood. It could change what it saw'; now, however, 'it looks the same way always, never swiveling for a child or a woman or the full feel of a breeze on its red face. Its stare is stiffly fixed on broken comrades, on glass. On a whole race of unwanteds.'

The relationship between consciousness and surface is, however, usually more complex – even crisis-laden – than is the case in 'The Red Chair'. In 'The Weather Sours and the Sweetness Is Good', for example, we find ourselves in a much more difficult relationship with the seen:

> He touched the table and felt recoil, the grains fleeing into themselves. He knew surfaces announced a litany of what he could never enter, a world forever cut off from him. They

would always elude his desires, they would disrobe for him,
allow the photo, admit to light and his fingers' promenade
– but nothing more.

Here the private life of the inanimate is seen as being forever inaccessible, as being merely a striptease in consciousness itself, one which leaves the observer in 'quite possibly the very sty of loneliness', as a later paragraph puts it – a place where perhaps the only reading matter is these poems, the allowed photos of the eluding world.

Many other poems hinge on this crisis of consciousness in the face of the seen, and it is maybe this that accounts for the number of poems about strangers. In *The Suspicious Sympathy of White*, fifteen of the sixty-one poems are concerned with watching strangers in such places as trains, coffee shops, or airports. (This compares with eleven poems in the same book about inanimate objects.) These people are typically seen from the outside and, insofar as they are approached, are only approached in the imagination. Sometimes the imagining is tinged with the erotic, but whether or not this is the case, it is the very inaccessibility of the stranger that is the driving force of the poem. If this sounds rather voyeuristic, in one sense it is, but the writing is always clear-sighted about to what degree the watching constitutes an awareness of an actual other and to what extent it is a stimulus to self-discovery.

Thus, in 'The Importance of Moisture', the speaker in the poem is sitting next to a woman who is reading a book on a train, 'the perfect stranger … hiding from me effortlessly.' He goes on to wonder whether 'the very book in her hand, from which she never once raised her eyes, was a foil, a cloak meant to ward me off.' If it is, it both does and does not succeed: 'She could not know of my love for theater. How for me a closed curtain is a rippling set of lips for which the only adequate response is trembling.' Here, it is the invisibility of the stranger's own inner drama, the very fact that the curtains are closed in front of the stage, that is the stimulus to the performance mounted in the speaker's imagination, one which culminates in the fantasy of 'our getting off the train together, entwined, leaving as partners, as if such deep involvement could spring fully bloomed and inexplicably watered.' But this fantasy soon enough runs up against a bleak recognition of its limits:

> But then I remembered that earlier in the morning I could not even get a stray kitten to drink from the bowl of chilled milk I had set out for it. A kitten who had been howling all night for moisture.

Earlier in the poem the speaker had been reading Proust on 'The Ephemeral Efficacy of Sorrow', an essay he dryly summarises as teaching that 'it seems gratitude is in order for those who grant us pain', an insight that helps dispel 'the morning fog enshrouding our hearts deep into the day'. At the end of the poem, the fog has dispersed and all is clear: the speaker knows that the kitten, although vulnerable, is unable to accept help for reasons that are inaccessible to any outsider; the perfect stranger on the train remains and will remain unknown; and the speaker is left, after the morning fogs have cleared, with a view of 'the heart stark in its solitude'.

Thus, the imaginings about strangers in these poems can sometimes be expressive only of the needs, desires and self-understandings of the speaker; it is significant that none of the observed people are aware of the attention being paid to them: they are asleep, reading, working, or otherwise engaged. Sometimes, however, fantasy is used as a means of approaching an intuition of the uniqueness of the other, of testing the possibility of presence and of understanding. In 'The Reception', an old man has fallen asleep sitting up on the train with 'his graceful thickly veined hands … curved upward on his lap'; these hands, the speaker comments, 'deserve to be met on even grounds, met halfway on their own terms, the terms of acceptance, but who among us is so qualified, so deserving?' The poem includes a notably surreal image ('I imagine his hands each with a palmful of eyes in them, the resting globes blinking languidly'), but the final emphases are, on the one hand, realist, focusing on the old man's vulnerability, the way he drools on his shirt, and 'his sweating bald pate ... rimmed by retreating hairs', and, on the other hand, sympathetic, with the speaker intuiting that as death begins its approach the old man has begun the process of dissolution of self and assimilation to something larger than individual existence: the old man 'has started moving outward, away from his center ... apparently [having] seen enough'. It is presumably life that he has seen enough of, and now, 'like the clouds when they part, he is making way for the moon, a thin sliver now beginning its rise on his ready and willing cranium.' Once again, the stranger is unaware of being observed, but here the focus is on what can be understood of the other, not of the self, through the act of observing.

❧

Silverstein does not, of course, write only about bricks, spoons, bread rolls, and perfect strangers. There are poems about known others, as in the playful, sexy and reciprocal scenario described in 'In Praise of Floods', where the speaker and a colleague, who share a rule – which includes a ban on kissing – that 'we shall not play Fountains', nevertheless embrace pleasurably on a regular basis when sharing an elevator. However, there are many poems where this kind of overt reciprocity is not on display – or perhaps it might be better to say where a different and more indirect kind of reciprocity can be seen at work. This tendency may, I think, have something to do with Silverstein's training as a psychologist and his work in Tokyo as a psychotherapist.

The conversation between client and therapist in a counselling session is not usually of the same kind as the reciprocal, unselfconscious interaction found in ordinary social exchanges. (In what follows I will refer to the therapist as 'he' and to the client as 'she' since that is the situation in the poem I will discuss below.) One of the therapist's roles is the highly self-conscious one of providing an open, non-threatening space within which the other may speak (to herself as much as to him) in such a way that the causes of her distress become clear to her. In order to do this, the therapist has to reduce attention to his own desires and distresses to a minimum, to avoid interventions arising from his personal self alone, to observe closely and objectively, and yet to use the full range of his imagination and experience in an attempt to intuit how the client may be experiencing, understanding, and misunderstanding her life. In other words, the therapist's role requires him both to abnegate his personal self yet to use all the social and imaginative skills that that self has developed (along with the skills developed during his professional training) to mirror back to the client what she is saying and what she might mean by what she is saying; the hope is that this unusual kind of 'conversation' may lead to emotional and psychological exploration, to intuitive understanding, and perhaps to liberation for the client.

Silverstein rarely writes directly about the therapeutic encounter. One exception to this, however, seems to be 'The Magnets of Paris Are Tired'. In this poem, the other is a woman 'whose thinness [is] veiled in unkempt red hair, a froth of self overwhelmed, or angry waves flooding her forehead with rage', someone who has 'spoken of succumbing to despair'. When she begins to talk about a blind boy and his grandmother who she has seen on a train, the therapist watches, listens, and notices that in the act of description she 'suddenly [comes] to life'. She describes the boy's ten fingers moving along his grandmother's face, 'a dance of touching but untouched porcelains, a gypsy caravan of equally tender virgins', and also describes 'the endless indulgence of she-who-could-see-so-well'.

This act of description (of two strangers) by the woman has a transformative effect on her: 'in describing all this, slowly and deliberately, this red being suddenly recovered luster, the snake had pulse!' The transformation seems complete, affecting everything from her red hair to the depths of the psyche that the therapist can imagine even if he will never be able to have access to them:

> the rest was inevitable, the pompadour retrieved its grace, the sea remembered its destiny, and the fish I could only imagine as being in the depths, sensed again the way back towards true north

This moment of reorientation, the therapist intuits, may allow her 'passage into [a] new and brighter room' and provide a 'clear hint of the more embracing life she wanted.'

It is significant that it is an act of description that leads to the reorientation, and that the poem draws specific attention to this: the woman 'in describing – that act – in describing his ghostly white skin ... [and] his fingers / moving along his grandmother's face' finds herself asking 'who can really trace gratitude adequately?' In the act of attention to unknown others, in the self-abnegation of her observing, in the attempt to intuit what the actions she is watching mean to those who are performing them, she is behaving rather like her therapist. Indeed, she is perhaps behaving rather like the writer of David Silverstein's poems: watching, imagining, and testing that imagining in such a way as to lead to insight into the other or the self. Reading this poem helps, I think, clarify the way in which his work as a psychotherapist and his play as a poet possibly affected and benefitted each other.

ࢋ

Almost all David Silverstein's best poetry is in the form of the prose poem; indeed, it's possible to say that he didn't fully find his voice until he discovered this form. His first book, *Dazzled by Nothing* (1984) consists of forty-three poems, of which only one is a prose poem, while his second, and strongest, book, *The Suspicious Sympathy of White* (1990) contains sixty-one poems, of which no less than fifty-four are prose poems; the balance is only slightly redressed in his final, short book *Apparitions* (1991), with seventeen poems in prose and nine in lines. If the books are read in order, there is a strong sense as one starts the second volume of a voice coming into its own, an achievement that is, I think, related to Silverstein's discovery that the sentence and the paragraph, rather than the line and the stanza, are his proper formal units.

The line was, of course, originally a metrical unit, but Silverstein in his early poems shows few signs of interest in this; if he sometimes seems to be settling down into an iambic trimeter or tetrameter, the pattern is soon enough ruffled and made irregular. In many ways this is not surprising for an American poet who leans towards non-traditional forms: 'to break the pentameter, that was the first heave,' said Ezra Pound in Canto LXXXI, and William Carlos Williams spent a lifetime trying to develop an alternative prosody responsive to the demands of a specifically American modernism. Silverstein sometimes skilfully uses one of the most successful techniques employed by Williams in his early poetry, the use of line ending and enjambment to lead the reader forward line by line through a series of small shocks of linguistic attention, as in the first stanza of 'The Silence Shared in Crevices':

> The tailor was deaf
> and dumb and spoke
> with the tip
> of his silver needle:
> finally precision

Here, there are a number of signs that we are reading the work of a poet who has paid attention to Williams: the surprise of the enjambment as the word 'dumb' is added to the apparently definitive syntax of the first line; the paradoxical surprise of the claim in the second line that the dumb tailor can after all speak; the momentary withholding of the resolution of this contradiction in the third line, along with the use of the word 'tip', with its echo of the expression 'on the tip of the tongue' (rather than 'point', a more usual collocation with 'needle'); the resolution of the contradiction with the discovery that what has a tip and speaks is the tailor's needle; and the comment in the fifth line – 'finally precision' – a line which refers equally to the precision of the tailor's art, to the achieved metaphor of sewing as speech, and to the deft handling of syntax, idiom, and enjambment in the stanza.

More often, however, the lines in *Dazzled by Nothing* seem neither to be conforming to traditional metre, nor to be playing speech rhythms against a ghostly underlying metrical norm, as recommended by T. S. Eliot in his 'Reflections on *Vers Libre*', nor even working in terms of a self-conscious play of syntax against line as in Williams. Here is a sentence by Silverstein:

> The silence serves as a moat and all the bridges are consumed with fire: only two words are needed to make a sentence, and but two souls to form a country, and the philosophers debate whether a guillotine falling in an empty room has really occurred, and whether the severed head staring from the corner was someone of principle.

If we compare this with the original, the last stanza of the lineated poem 'Allegiance' (on page 18 in this selection), how much has been lost by rewriting it as prose?

> the silence serves as a moat
> and all the bridges are consumed
> with fire: only two words are needed
> to make a sentence, and but two souls

> to form a country and the philosophers
> debate whether a guillotine falling
> in an empty room has really occurred
> and whether the severed head
> staring from the corner
> was someone of principle.

We lose the surprise of the enjambment 'consumed / with fire', to be sure, but otherwise there seems to be little damage done, the passage making its considerable impact rather from the strength of its final image than from its metrical movement; and this strength comes over, I feel, with as much, or perhaps even more, force in the prose version as in the lineated original.

Thus, Silverstein's thoroughgoing commitment to the prose poem in his second book may simply be due to the discovery that that was the form he had been wanting to use all along, and that the institution of the line was an inhibition to the flow of his writing; the speed of his transitions, already quite quick in his first book, is considerably faster in his second, where the absence of line endings allows him to just keep on going if he wants to. Certainly, there's an almost palpable sense of relief as he settles into the prose poem form at the beginning of *The Suspicious Sympathy of White*. The poem with which he chose to begin that book, 'The Pig', is an extraordinary performance; I'm not sure how successful it finally is as a poem, but it certainly covers a lot of ground: Moscow in winter, the 'cheap vinyl exterior' of a pig, Maine in August (complete with blueberries), the difficulties that afflict a pig shopping for a negligee or heels, art students drawing a nude, the sexually excited pig as 'a theoretical mathematician of lust', and the Moscow snow covering 'a lost city of stone men, buried busts of Stalin' which are seen as being like 'huge slugs gathering strontium'. If it sounds as if all these things might not hang together in a single poem, I think that perhaps they don't. On the other hand, this gleefully baggy, yet inventive and linguistically fast-moving piece of writing suggests that formal perfection, the sense of completion or of having reached a definitive conclusion, were not the sort of things that Silverstein was after; rather he wanted the improvisational freedom to go wherever the encounter between his perceptions and his language was taking him, and to go there fast. One never knows where a Silverstein poem is going to go next; he is less a sculptor than a downhill skier or a surfer, and the reader, rather than being asked to engage with an artistic object, is – exhilaratingly – taken along for the ride.

❧

David Lehman, in the introduction to his anthology *Great American Prose Poems: From Poe to the Present* (2003), has said that if you are a poet writing in prose 'you give up much, but you gain in relaxation, in the possibilities of humor and incongruity, in narrative compression, and in the feeling of escape or release from tradition or expectation'. I think all of these are reasons why the form suited Silverstein so well; as a man and as a writer he was relaxed and humorous (with a particular taste for the incongruous), liked narrative, and, as a psychotherapist, was deeply interested in release from inhibition or oppressive expectations.

However, the attraction of the prose poem for Silverstein can, I think, be more precisely specified in three ways. The first of these is that the prose poem is perhaps the ideal form for the expression of the experience of the *flâneur*. Baudelaire, the earliest significant writer of prose poems, speaks in 'Crowds', the twelfth of his *Petits Poèmes en prose*, of 'the gift of enjoying a crowd-bath', of the poet as he 'luxuriat[es] in the throng' enjoying 'the unique privilege of being himself and other people, at will', and claims that 'the thoughtful perambulating loner derives a special kind of uplift from this communion with all and sundry'. The Tokyo conurbation with its crowds and its enormous population (31 million), its emphasis on public rather than private transport, and its local walkability is perhaps the ideal city for the modern *flâneur*, and Silverstein's poems often take off from something glimpsed in a Tokyo street: 'The Ignored Bird', 'Thinking of the Few Scattered Shells I'd Keep on My Desk Afterwards', 'The Brick', 'The Red Chair', and 'The Dry Teat' are all examples, and he has also made several significant contributions ('The Importance of Moisture' and 'The Reception', for instance) to what has almost become a Tokyo poetic genre, the 'someone-seen-on-a-train' poem. All these poems seem good examples of what Baudelaire described as the soul yielding itself 'in all its poetry and all its charity to the epiphany of the unforeseen, the unknown passer-by' (translations of Baudelaire by Francis Scarfe).

A second reason that the prose poem may have appealed to Silverstein perhaps lies in the association of the form with surrealism, and thus its openness to the psychological insights that might be gained by recourse to the unconscious or through the articulation of fantasy. David Lehman reports a quip that if you say *prose poem* in a word association game, the next word that is likely to come to everybody's mind is *surreal* or *surrealist*; and indeed there is a long tradition of the surrealist or surrealism-influenced prose poem in twentieth-century French literature, dating back to such books as André Breton's *Clair de terre* (1923) and *Le Revolver aux cheveux blancs* (1932). Lehman also quotes Michael Benedikt, the editor of the first anthology of prose poems to be published in America, *The Prose Poem: An International Anthology* (1976), as saying that 'there is a shorter distance from the unconscious to the Prose Poem than from the unconscious to most poems in verse'. In this, Benedikt is following in the footsteps of Robert Bly, who in an essay argues that the prose poem is a form particularly supportive of poetic 'leaping', which 'can be described as a leap from the conscious to the unconscious and back again, a leap from the known part of the mind to the unknown part and back to the known'. Stephen Fredman, in his *Poet's Prose: The Crisis in American Verse* (1990) describes this position – that the prose poem inherently provides a royal road to the unconscious – as 'nonsensical', pointing out that 'unconscious forces are at work in any human creation'; however, although this objection is certainly theoretically valid, there nevertheless is a canon and a tradition in which the prose poem is closely linked with the unconscious and the surreal, with dream and fantasy, and it also seems reasonable that writing in prose should be more likely to lead to free association in a psychological sense than if the writer is required to pay attention to the formal requirements of verse. Given the history and achievements of the form, and its bias towards the psychological and the surreal, it is easy to see why a professional psychotherapist with a PhD in child psychology would want to explore it.

The third, and I think crucial reason for Silverstein's interest in the prose poem is something I mentioned earlier: the form's openness to improvisation. Writing about William Carlos Williams's *Kora in Hell* (1920) – a work significantly subtitled *Improvisations* – Stephen Fredman says that 'to speak of one's work as improvisation is to emphasise the spontaneous over the planned, the discovery of form over the formal contract, the new over the traditional'; he then goes on to quote Gerard L. Bruns, also writing about Williams: 'An improvisation is a piece of unforeseen discourse. One cannot predict anything about it. It is discourse that makes no provision for a future.' All this sounds very much like a description of a Silverstein prose poem. This is not to say that that he never revised or re-wrote – I suspect that he did – but the emphasis on the moment, on flow, on the discovery of the unexpected, are keys to his writing, I believe. This approach is best summed up in a paragraph by Fredman about Williams, which could equally well apply to Silverstein's work:

> [T]he improvisation has about it a certain timeliness, the stamp of a specific moment. It purports to be the farthest thing from a timeless utterance; it is a meditation upon the

moment, with the implication that no further revision is possible. First and foremost a beginning, an improvisation begins from the middle, not from a point of origin.... [T]he text continues beginning throughout its length, abjuring the sense of finality through contradiction, paradox, and non sequitur. An improvisation differs from a work of fiction or argument in that the latter two, from the beginning, tend towards an end, while the improvisation tends to go on. An improvisation ends not when it has attained a necessary formal or thematic completion but when it has played itself out.

Silverstein's engagement with the unexpected, whether on the street, in a train, in his kitchen, or in his consulting room always gives the impression of beginning *in medias res* and of flowing forward rapidly, of exploring, of finding out what can be discovered through imaginative play, and then, once insight (rather than formal or thematic completion) has been achieved, stopping. Regardless of whether or not in practice he re-wrote or revised, this immediacy of effect was what I think he was aiming at. In this his work has some similarities with jazz, the excitement of which, as Fredman observes, 'comes from being present (as musician or listener) at the moment of creation'.

In a prose poem the sentence and the paragraph act the roles taken by the line and the stanza in poems written in verse, and Silverstein's handling of the sentence is very various, ranging from the minimalist phrase to the paragraph-long, subordinated sentence. He can cover a considerable distance in a sentence, as in this one, from 'Ginger Mousse', a poem not selected here: 'Once glimpsed by the throat childhood fades from the cheeks of leaves and the leaves are drained of illusion are themselves.' The flicker – and progression – of associations in these words is quite startling: a glimpse, a murderous grab by the throat leading to the loss of colour in the cheeks of the child, which turn out to be leaves, which makes the child part of nature as the sap of illusion drains from leaves and cheeks alike into a necessary, identity-defining disillusion. The theme is Wordsworthian – or the sentence could even perhaps be seen as a twenty-one-word secular version of Gerard Manley Hopkins's 'Spring and Fall'.

Similarly, his paragraphs can build on an idea through a series of images and then suddenly switch tracks so that reader is shunted to an entirely unpredicted destination:

> The ends of string remain strangers. They live through rumor of each other. Tension frenzy ripple and the occasional false passion of the knot, the electrical grip insuring the climber's greed: I want to lick the summit, I want to imprison the vista, I want to see the world from above as I do my cuffs.

The move, in this paragraph from 'The Weather Sours and the Sweetness Is Good', from the conceit of the two ends of a piece of string being individuals who are unaware of each other yet are part of the same continuum, through the illusion of sexual connection between them ('the occasional false passion of the knot'), which insures (makes safe, and presumably also ensures and legitimates) their greed, which is like that of the mountaineer protected by the knot in his climbing rope, who suddenly steps out of the sentence to speak *in propria persona* of his triumph and his imperialist aesthetic project in the full complacency of his self-regard as he looks down on the (presumably nicely laundered and crisply starched) cuffs of his own expensive shirt. This is quite a journey. I am aware that my description of the paragraph is longer than the paragraph itself, and that I have imported some details (Silverstein says nothing about the cost of his speaker's shirt, for example), but this is done in an attempt to convey the suggestive richness, the speed, and the excitement of what the paragraph offers me as it races past.

Not all of Silverstein's prose poems maintain this degree of linguistic density all the way through, but some of them are powerfully sustained over many paragraphs. An example is 'Living Alone', which begins:

> Again the unexpected lodge in which all of life is turned into a throat. Beneath ground the stalled train in the unwet vestibule. The saliva is gone. We can no longer swallow, there is no desire, as if all intentions were ludicrous and we realised it simultaneously. Could this shaft be the long inverted finger of the netherworld beckoning, the invitation I have longed to find in my path?

The first sentence is very striking, if not at first easily interpretable; it is only when in the second sentence we realise we are in a stationary train between stations in the Tokyo metro system that the metaphor of the tunnel being like a parched throat becomes clear, and that it also becomes clear that the conceit is working as an emblem of the failure of desire. The unexpected words 'lodge' (implying both a temporary state of dwelling and something 'lodged in the throat') and 'vestibule' (an anonymous portal) both suggest the alienated nature of our inhabitation of this place 'where nothing is supposed to happen and only nothing thrives', as the second paragraph puts it. This text, the end of the first paragraph makes clear, is going to be a journey to the underworld.

There is, however, no Tiresias, no Virgil, here to act as a guide. Marooned in 'this ungodly place which should be a vertical drop but isn't', and which 'matches no station and thus on maps-of-aspiration does not exist', the speaker notices through the window a steel bolt embedded in the tunnel wall and becomes fascinated by it. This 'massive single bolt becomes the sun'; it 'overwhelms' the speaker, who 'assume[s] its tightness', noticing the way in which 'these irregular metals facing belly to belly are clasped, not roughly, but the adherence seem[ing] almost liquid in its merge.' This is, once more, one of Silverstein's anthropomorphic explorations of the life and psyche of an object, but this time the understanding, as befits insight into an inhabitant of the netherworld, is a desolating one:

> Suddenly I feel the desolation of the bolt, the terrible loveliness of such twisted loyalty endlessly waiting for a dawn which does not break. Its surrender to the wrench and strange appeal of rust on cheeks whose autumnal flush cannot be stroked. And the slow clouding over of the bolt's one eye until it huddles blind around itself each time the plunging beast returns. Engulfed by a terrible wind which demands the worship of held breath.

The bolt's 'twisted loyalty', 'its surrender to the wrench', 'the slow clouding over of the bolt's one eye until it huddles blind around itself' – all these are powerful and compassionate images of a tragically stoic innocence trapped in the timeless hell of the underworld. The poem ends: 'In such a world as this the howl is all, and dreams of lubricant derange a small metallic mind.'

This is perhaps Silverstein's fiercest and most desolate poem. But it must be remembered that he can also be an extremely funny poet (in 'Invasion of the Room Snatchers', for instance) and also a marvellous poet of happiness. In 'The Walk', a poem set in Ubud, in the interior of Bali, the speaker goes for a walk 'through the terraced ripple of the rice paddies and high wild grass swaying like dry water'.

> The path climbs. I head for the house in a cluster of trees. Luka is there. Luka gives me tea. She gives me welcome. I do not know her. I know her. There are books here I would have chosen for myself. And the mats and the art and the view, the posture taken by the house. I don't remember calling ahead. Is it possible that my heart leads a private life of its own, a life even I don't know?

This is one of my favourite poems about the heart-restoring (and, of course, temporary) sense of paradise that is from time to time available to us in a world more often devoted to surrendering to the wrench – a smiling, evocative record of one of those days on which everything feels right:

> A chicken struts at my feet. Above me a bee enters the home
> it has made in a wooden dragon hanging by a single thread.
> The wind playfully making it a little harder.

Paul Rossiter

www.ingramcontent.com/pod-product-compliance
Lightning Source LLC
Chambersburg PA
CBHW031204090426
42736CB00009B/779